Kids and Money
The 5 Stacks Method!

by

Nadia Cropley

&

Ramat Oyetunji

Published by Tinu Publishing, LLC
Published in the USA
ISBN: 978-0-9863204-1-5
Copyright 2021
All rights reserved.

*This book is dedicated to kids everywhere.
I hope you explore different things, find the ones
you love and the ones that make you happy.
Remember to spread kindness every day!*

Hi! My name is Nadia, and this book is about how I use The 5 Stacks Method to manage the money I earn from my car cleaning business.

I hope you stick around till the end of the book. I share how I started my business and what I have learned. But first, let me tell you how I started using this simple way of managing money.

One night, a few weeks after I started my business, I asked my Mom to tell me a bedtime story. There was a catch. It had to be a story she made up herself! She is good at using her imagination, so I love asking her to make up stories just for me. That is how I learned about Kemi and her 5 stacks of money.

~ o ~

"Once upon a time, there was a girl called Kemi. She had just started a business and earned $90 in the first week. Kemi was excited about making so much money, but she did not want to spend it all or lose it. After thinking for a while, she came up with an idea. She would split her money into 5 stacks.

💡 Stack #1: Kemi was a kind girl who liked helping others, so she decided she would use her first stack of money for donations to charity.

💡 Stack #2: Kemi knew that she would have to buy more supplies for her business, and maybe even make some posters, if she wanted to get new customers to keep her business growing. She decided to use her second stack of money to grow her business.

💡 Stack #3: Kemi loved playing Roblox and was on her way to being a pro (or at least not a noob!) She decided to use her third stack of money to give herself a treat for working so hard. She bought some Robux and used it to upgrade her avatar.

💡 Stack #4: Kemi knew that she should save some of the money in case she wanted to use it in the future. She decided to put her fourth stack of money in her piggy bank. Later, her Mom or Dad would put it in her savings account at the bank.

💡 Stack #5: Kemi had heard her Mom talking about investing in companies. She thought it would be cool to invest in Roblox, her favorite gaming company. She happily told her friends she was a Roblox shareholder.

As Kemi's business grew and she earned more money, she still used The 5 Stacks Method. The end."

~o~

While my Mom was telling the story, I imagined myself as Kemi. When she got to the end of the story, I said: "Mom! I am going to manage my money using 5 Stacks, just like Kemi!"

💡 How would you split your 5 stacks? Equal stacks or different size stacks?

THE 5 STACKS

#5 Investing

#4 Saving

#1 Giving

#3 Spending

#2 Growing

STACK #1: GIVING

Are you thinking "Hey! I just earned this money, and now I have to give it away?!"

That was my first thought too! But after I thought about it, I realized that I was just like Kemi; I also like helping others, and it makes me feel happy.

I used some of the money in my GIVING stack to buy groceries for a local group. They feed families in need within our community. I also donated money to another local group. They help parents in need buy gifts for their kids during the holidays.

Cool reasons to have a GIVING stack

- 💡 You are helping others within your community and in other places.
- 💡 Helping others makes your community stronger and better.
- 💡 Helping others feels good!

Phrase to remember "What goes around comes around!"

💡 What do you think it means?

ACTIVITY

1. Think of 2 reasons why giving is important to you personally. Share those reasons with your family and friends.

   Giving is important to me because

   _____

   _____

2. Write the name of 2 local groups that help people in your community. How do they help?

   Two groups helping people in my community are

   _____

   _____

   They help by

   _____

CREATIVE SPACE

Write, doodle, or draw your ideas!

STACK #2: GROWING

The second stack is about growing. Growing could mean growing your business, like I plan to do, or it can mean growing your skills.

For example, if you earn some money by making bracelets, you could improve your skills by taking a bracelet-making class.

Cool reasons to have a GROWING stack

- 💡 It allows you to continue doing a good job. For example, for my business, my GROWING stack will help me buy more supplies. I can then continue to do a good job cleaning cars and making my customers happy.

- 💡 It allows you to improve what you are doing so that you can be even better. For example, I used some of the money in my growing stack for a new idea. My customers could choose from 3 types of car fresheners after I cleaned their car. That made them happy, which means they will keep coming back!

Phrase to remember "Rome was not built in a day!"

- 💡 What do you think it means?

ACTIVITY

1. Think of 2 things you did, or used, that helped you earn money. What are they?

   Two things that helped me earn money are

   _____

   _____

2. How can you improve the 2 things you mentioned above so that they continue to help you earn money?

   I can improve by

   _____

   _____

3. How else can you improve?

   _____

CREATIVE SPACE
Write, doodle, or draw your ideas!

STACK #3: SPENDING

The FUN part! After working so hard, I am sure you can't wait to spend some money on something you want.

It is okay to spend some of your money on something that you are excited about, even if no one else is excited about it!

Guess what I bought with some of my SPENDING money? Robux (just like Kemi!) and a drawing pad with colored pencils.

Cool reasons to have a SPENDING stack

- 💡 Spending some of your money on something you like makes you feel rewarded for your hard work.
- 💡 It makes you feel independent because you are making smart decisions about what to buy and how to budget!
- 💡 You help other businesses to thrive and keep the economy going.

Phrase to remember "All work and no play makes Jack a dull boy."

- 💡 What do you think it means?

ACTIVITY

1. Think of 2 ways you would reward yourself for your hard work. Tell your family and friends about your choices. Are they surprised?

   I would reward myself by

   _____

   _____

2. If you don't have enough money to spend on something you really want, what would you do?

   I would

   _____

   _____

3. Discuss your choices from #2 with your family or friends. What advice did they give you?

   _____

CREATIVE SPACE

Write, doodle, or draw your ideas!

STACK #4: SAVING

If you are like me, you have at least one piggy bank. My favorite one is actually a kitty bank, which I made in an art class. It is very cute!

The fourth stack is for your piggy bank, but you don't really have to stuff your piggy bank; you are old enough to have a savings account at a bank. I was excited when my parents took me to a bank to open up my very own account. I felt like such a grown-up!

Cool reasons to have a SAVING stack

- 💡 It is a great way to plan for a big expense. For example, planning for a special birthday or Christmas gift for your Mom or Dad.

- 💡 It comes in handy if something unexpected happens. For example, if you lost something important to you and you want to replace it without asking your Mom or Dad for the money.

Phrase to remember "Save for a rainy day!"

- 💡 What do you think it means?

ACTIVITY

1. Think of 2 reasons why saving some of your money is important to you personally. Share those reasons with your family or friends.

   Saving is important to me because

   _____

   _____

2. Think of the places you could keep your money safe.

   I can keep my money safe in

   _____

3. Write the name of 2 local banks or credit unions in your community. What do they do?

   _____

CREATIVE SPACE

Write, doodle, or draw your ideas!

STACK #5: INVESTING

We are finally at the last stack! What is investing?

I learned that investing is about using your money to create, build or improve. For example, you could invest money in a business to create, build or improve that business. When the business grows and makes more money, your money (investment) grows too.

Cool reasons to have an INVESTING stack

- 💡 You are part of creating, building or improving something.

- 💡 It helps you support businesses or causes that you believe in. This type of investing is called Socially Responsible Investing.

- 💡 It helps you grow the money that you already have, which you can then use for other important things.

Phrase to remember "It takes money to make money!"

- 💡 What do you think it means?

ACTIVITY

1. Think of 2 ways you could invest your money. Discuss it with your parents.

   I can invest some of my money by
   _____

   _____

2. What are 2 things you would want to know before investing your money in a business?

   I would want to know
   _____

   _____

3. How could you learn more about a business before investing your money?

   I could learn more about a business by
   _____

CREATIVE SPACE
Write, doodle, or draw your ideas!

SAVING vs INVESTING

SAVING and INVESTING seem to have the same idea behind them, but they are not the same thing.

SAVING	INVESTING
💡 Keep your money in a safe place for a rainy day. You may earn some interest, but your money will not grow very much.	💡 Grow your money by using your money to create, build or improve something that grows in value. For example, buying the shares of a company you believe in. You become a shareholder (owner) and as the company grows successful, the value of your shares increases.
💡 Easy to access, in case you need it for an emergency or unexpected expense.	💡 Not easy to access because your money is being used to create, build or improve the business you invested in!

SPOT THE DIFFERENCE!

Read the 2 scenarios below and determine which one is an example of SAVING and which is an example of INVESTING. How did you decide? Explain your choice to your family or a friend.

- 💡 Scenario 1: You have $20 and put it in a savings account which earns interest and increases to $20.20 at the end of the year.

  _____

- 💡 Scenario 2: You and your friend each have $20. You buy $40 worth of supplies for a lemonade stand. At the end of the week, you each get $30 from selling lemonade.

  _____

A FINAL WORD FROM NADIA

The idea for a car cleaning business occurred to me one summer afternoon when my Mom and I were walking around our neighborhood. I was 8, but my 9th birthday was in a few weeks.

My Mom was disappointed with how messy her car was, and she said I would be the one to clean it since it was mostly my mess. I was looking forward to playing Roblox after our walk, so I was not excited at all about cleaning her car instead.

As we continued on our walk, I started thinking of how I could turn cleaning my Mom's car into a business. I shared some of my ideas with her, and she loved them!

- 💡 I told her that first, we would sign a contract.

- 💡 I asked her to tell me what she expected for a job well done and how much she would pay me.

- 💡 Because I knew how messy her car was, I told her that I would take a break if it took longer than one hour!

When we got home from our walk, I immediately gathered all the things I needed to clean my Mom's car. I wiped, dusted, and vacuumed for about 2 hours. It was hard work! When I finished, my Mom was happy and gave me a big tip.

That is how my car cleaning business was born. I even wrote a business plan and came up with a slogan:

"Car a mess? Don't stress!"

5 IMPORTANT LESSONS I LEARNED

- 💡 Not everything is going to be easy at first. I realized that when I had to clean a big SUV that was very messy and full of dog hair. It was more work than my Mom's car!

- 💡 Sometimes you have to be ready to do the job even if you don't feel like it. One day I didn't want to clean a customer's car because I was feeling lazy. But I did it anyway because I had said I was going to do it.

- 💡 Always make your customers happy. Customers are the best, and they give you tips if they are satisfied with your work.

- 💡 I learned that I should always put money aside for later. You never know when you will need it.

- 💡 I learned that it is important to communicate with your customers so that there isn't any confusion. You can do it by email or an app like calendly. I use both (my Mom helps me!)

If you were to start a business, what type of business would it be?

_____

_____

Follow me on Instagram!
@the.fi.kid

Made in the USA
Middletown, DE
18 January 2022